World wide carrier opportunities

Index

1. Enterprise Education

2. Food Stylist

3. Event Management

4. Fashion

5. N.R.I Banking

6. Fire Engineering

7. Food Production

8. Video Editing

9. Foreign Language

10. Medical Lab Technician

11. Architect

12. International Business

13. Dietitian and Nutrionnist

14. stenographer

15. Dentist

16. Veterinarian

17. Tourism

18. Radiologic and MRI technologist

19. Pilot

20. Software Developer

1. Enterprise education

Today the country needs skilled workers in Engineer Research Accountancy and hundreds of other departments, however the most needed is they include business leaders and visionaries, who have a clear vision of setting up a future business, considering India's vast size and population, there is a lack of better governance and excellent

management companies in India .
These companies are important
because it gives an invaluable
contribution to the economy .With
this, jobs are available, economic
conditions are also strong. The job
market of India is a period of
uncertainty. Many graduates in the
country are unlikely to get jobs .
That's why young Indians need to be
allocated to work. There is a need
for a new generation of businessmen
in India who understand business and
earn money. It is such a thing which
does not need much education for
which the next generation Business
leaders must have good education and
training in good arts to talk to
people with confidence.

How Business Education Will Build
Business Leaders?

It is a bit difficult and
challenging to study
entrepreneurship compared to taking
education from other subjects
because those who are trained to
become businessmen should have some
good qualities and different

qualities apart from others .
However, enterprise dispensation
should be taken only by those people
who have special qualities. Today's
demand is to emerge the
businesswomen who can take advantage
of new ways to take advantage of new
techniques and business by providing
practical and profitable business
enterprises vacations. Spreading
more teaches tricks to start your
business as a practical idea and to
make it successful

Advantages of Enterprise Education

Almost every school or college in
India gives grades of students.
These great shows that the students
will be admitted to the college
university for higher education in
their future . It also shows that in
the field of education in the
future, where the students will be
employed, the enterprise vacation
college education in some way has
passed or failed students with real
life education . By teaching the
real life in the way of teaching,
enterprise education teaches

students to take lessons from their successes and failures, in reality people learn in this manner.

## What Does Enterprise Education Teach?

Enterprise education prepares people to start their own business, to run a business, to identify the problems encountered in real life and to overcome these problems, thinking strategically should have the ability to consider it . To run a business, a business should also think seriously about the solution in order to deal with any problem and challenge. A businessman should also understand the benefits of new technology or remember that the success of any business Innovation has been printed only. Businessman should constantly experiment with new innovation, Apart from this, enterprise education also teaches students how to achieve a common goal, all people can work together and in what way a person can work towards achieving any goal alone. for coming from the school mentioned above, the enterprise also teach these students. C it is taking responsibility to others the business sector can be bent Enterprise education to students how to see it and how to take responsibility for the consequences of their actions and deeds . Apart from this, enterprise education also teaches students how to achieve a common goal, all people can work together and in what way a person can work towards achieving any goal alone.

2.Food stylist

Nowadays, the hospitality industry of the country abroad is increasing rapidly and given the continuous opening of international hotels and restaurant chains in countries, it can be said that in this field the job officers are also increasing this field Part of the food stylist , The area of styling was limited to a few years before the film was printed or food packaging but food and Due to increasing business in the entertainment industry, the demand for food stylists has increased in this area.

What is food styling?

Often television commercials, restaurants and food magazines have seen such food items, which have been dashed to eat . It is amazing for the presentation which is called food styling, in it creates a beautiful image together with the food stylish photographer . In the film or TV industry, you can also see the wonderful career of office career.

This is work

According to Aruna Singh, principal of the Delhi Paramedical and Management Institute, a food stylist decorates food items in such a way that your mind immediately starts to buy or buy them. This work requires a lot of effort and creativity, it is the responsibility of the food stylists to buy food items and decorative items from shopping to prepare food.

3. Event management

The task of event management is to connect different types of tasks at the right time and with complete accuracy, which, according to the client, at the given time and in the given budget, without any hassle or accident, the most successful event manager . The pressure of time always stays with the pull of quality, and despite everything being fine, there is scope for reducing the deficit. Prior to organizing the event, when you celebrate the budget, you are about to celebrate the celebrity, you But this is an essential part of this work which can be both comfort and money by the completion of the work.

Skills

Different types of qualities are needed in the work of event management, and continuing to work, they continue to improve . Whether Leadership skills are quality or love or marketing, people make, Scale and Risk Management people work in all the stages and they continue to accumulate in them Every person who wants to join event management, It should be aware that what kind of skills are there in which they need to read in this work and without whom the non-sense decision can be made without first knowing it The entry in the field of Entry did not need any special qualifications or studies but has now opened the way for studies . If you have passed 12th, then you can do a degree or diploma in it.

Courses

Its main course is Diploma in Event Management, PG Diploma in Management, Advance Diploma in event Management and PR, pg Diploma in event Management and Activation . Under these courses, you can find liner servicing and presentation skills, set designing, event planning, and costing , Event Branding Production and Technology, Celebrities and Artist Management, Media Management, Sponsorship, Public Relations and Marketing, etc.

Salary

In the beginning, even though you get salary from 10 to 15000 only, due to hard work and effort, your salary may also be in lakhs

4. Fashion

Eligibility

Candidates must have a Graduate Post Graduate Diploma or Degree from a recognized institution. In this field, the student who does PhD in the field is given two preference. Candidates should have 4 to 5 years experience

Duration of course........
Duration of this course is 2 years and in addition the candidates can also do other short time courses.

Where you can get jobs?

After doing a fashion designing course, there are good opportunities for employment in Fashion House Manufacturing Units.

## 5. N.r.i banking

Who are N.R.I Banker?

According to Amit Goyal, director of PKW Institute of Banking Finance, there is always demand for NRI Bank in any government and private bank. An NRI Bank makes the provision of service to the NRI Client of that institute, which also helps the client get loan and also contributes to the investment process. NRI banker tells NRI customers about the ups and downs in services like internet rate, exchange rate, etc.

Courses...

In order to pursue a career in NRI Banking, candidates can complete PG Diploma in banking and finance after completing graduation from any field, this is a 1 year course in which the Banking Subjects like banking operations finance management trade finance are taught in this course, in this course, the students will be able to reduce their business with basic knowledge of computer and software as well as Knowledge of how Communication and Stock Market works.

Eligibility???
Graduated students and graduates from any Supreme year can apply for PG Diploma in Banking and Finance courses, and NRI Bank can take their first step towards becoming Bank. Even graduation with 50% marks from the screen is required.


Salary?...
Salary for NRI banker is up to 40-50 thousand INR Per month

# 6. FIRE ENGINEERING

## Nature of work

Joining fire department is a successful career as well as public service. The main task of fire fighter is to find out the reason for the fire and to analyze the measures to stop it. Fire fighting is an are related to civil, electrical, environmental engineering.

## Educational qualification

More individual qualification is required in this area as it is necessary in the field. Fire factories can be caught in fire and chemical factories, etc.
Still, for admission to the degree or diploma, it is necessary to pass

the 12th, even for some posts, the degree of fire is mandatory.

Physical qualification

In addition to academic qualification, the ability of the body to make a career in the field is also determined, the courage for men is 165 cm, 50 kg weight, the length of women should be at least 157 cm and weight should be at least 46 kg. Both Vision should be 6/6 for 19 years to 23 years of age.

Courses

Diploma in fire and safety , PG diploma in fire and safety , BSC in fire engineering , certificate courses in fire fighting fire technology and industrialist safety management , fire fighting etc are types of courses

7. Food production

Nature of work

Food production is to be cooked at any nation, hotel, fast food joint or any food stall. The role of the Food Production Manager does not end here. I do a new plane, make stuff, supervise the preparation, instruct the staff of the kitchen. Giving is also included in his responsibilities. Preparing a delicious meal of good quality is his religion because on the basis of which the customer If food comes, then food business will run, food production managers have different types of dishes and information about how to prepare them. A variety of production and service jobs exist in the food industry, ranging from cooking and culinary preparation to produce warehouse management. Food production service workers may be employed at full-service and fast-food restaurants, cafeterias, schools, hospitals, nonprofit organizations, government agencies, storage facilities and farms. Training typically focuses on food and preparation, while advanced studies often equip graduates for supervisory positions. Specific occupational options may include cook, chef, food supplier, banquet manager, purchasing manager or food production director, among others.

Chefs/Head Cooks
Food Service Managers
Waiters/Waitresses
Required Education
High school diploma and on-the-job experience
High school diploma plus long-term work experience

Entry level; Short-term on-the-job training
Other Requirements
Culinary arts school or postsecondary education preferred
Postsecondary education preferred
No formal education necessary
Projected Job Growth (2014-2024)
9%*
5%*
3%*

Average Salary (2015)
$45,920*
$53,640*
$23,020*

Source: *U.S. Bureau of Labor Statistics
Food Service Certification Options
Food service workers at all levels have the option of gaining certification through professional organizations or government agencies, such as the National Restaurant Association Educational Foundation, the American Culinary Federation or a state's department of health. Directors, kitchen staff, sanitation workers and culinary

professionals can earn credentials that demonstrate a level of knowledge and skill that meets industry standards. These certifications are not usually required for career entry, but could provide opportunities for advancement or greater income.

Food Service Education Requirements

Those looking to launch a food service career can find a number of educational options through public and private institutions. Many culinary schools or technical institutions prepare students for kitchen supervision, cooking or baking professions. Community colleges and universities offer degree options in hospitality, culinary studies or food service management at the undergraduate and graduate levels. Those interested in becoming a server, line cook or kitchen aide could earn a certificate in food service management through a college or vocational school, though some establishments hire high school graduates for several entry-level positions.

Food Service Technical Diploma
Diploma programs typically take a year to complete and offer the shortest route to start a career in the food service industry. Common courses include food principles, nutrition and food production.

Associate Degree in Culinary Arts
Associate degree programs typically provide a mix of food preparation and cooking skills for aspiring food service workers. These 2-year programs offer courses in business management and employee relations, as well as food preparation, sanitation and nutrition.

Bachelor's Degree in Food Service Management or Culinary Arts
A 4-year bachelor's degree program includes industry-specific education. Courses in a hospitality management program prepare graduates for supervisory positions in the industry, and teach business skills -- such as accounting and marketing -- aimed at restaurant, hotel and resort management. Culinary arts courses focus on food production, nutrition, purchasing and kitchen management.

Master's Degree in Food Science or Hospitality Management
Graduate programs at the master's level are sometimes offered either completely or partially online. Core and elective courses might focus on food research or restaurant management. Topics may include produce distribution and purchasing, food preparation, nutritional studies and employee supervision.
Salary and Job Outlook
Salaries in the field of food production and service can vary substantially by career. For example, according to the U.S. Bureau of Labor Statistics (BLS), chefs and head cooks made an average salary of $45,920 as of May 2015; whereas food preparation workers made an average yearly wage of $22,050 during that same reporting interval. Also as of May 2015, per the BLS, food service managers made an average salary of $53,640; while waiters and waitresses made an average of $23,020 per year. Employment projections are equally varied. For instance, the BLS projected that the number of

employed chefs and head cooks would grow by roughly 9% from 2014-2024, somewhat faster than average for all occupations. Meanwhile, the BLS estimated that the total number of food service managers was expected to change 5%, about as fast as the average within the same decade; while the number of waiters and waitresses was expected to grow by about 3%, still slower than average across occupations. Overall, the BLS projected that employment of food and beverage serving and related workers would grow approximately 10% from 2014 to 2024, generally faster than average across all occupations. With a high school diploma or hands-on experience, you can enter into a career in food production services. For those who are looking for managerial positions or long-term careers, pursuing an advanced degree in culinary arts is optional but not required. The annual salaries for food production and service jobs vary in range, with some workers earning a little over $23,000 and others earning close to $54,000 each year.

## 8. Video editing

Video editing

**VIDEO EDITOR**
Video editors employ digital and creative technology skills to assemble raw recorded material into a cohesive format, suitable for distribution. This post-production process is often believed to "make or break" a project; hence outstanding video editing is one of the arts recognized in prestigious entertainment awards and festival. What Is Video Editing?

Imagine yourself in a dim movie theater, your eyes riveted on the screen. While you were transfixed to the screen, you may have never noticed how seamlessly each scene blended into the next one, or how perfectly the sound effects and dramatic music fit into each part of the film. Now, wrap your mind around this - not one movie ever started out in this perfect seamless condition. When shooting a movie, cinematographers are not magical wizards that are able to get the perfect shot every time, and actors are not so perfect that they never make mistakes. Although an average movie is no longer than an hour and a half, each one typically starts out with hours and hours of raw footage. Video editing is the process of choosing the best raw footage for a movie. This includes removing unusable footage and stringing together what's left into the best possible sequence. Unusable footage often includes footage where actors make mistakes, the camera angles weren't just right, or it doesn't move the story forward somehow.

During the video editing process, each scene should segue into the next flawlessly. Sound is another important part of video editing. For example, sound effect may be added to the movie at just the right times, in order to make it appear as if they were part of the original video. This can include sound effects like explosions or even simple footsteps. Background music is often added as well.

Work Environment

A video editor is the professional responsible for editing the raw footage shot during the making of a movie. Before the increased use of more modern digital video cameras, movie footage was shot on real strips of film. Video editors had to physically cut and splice certain scenes together. Today, however, the majority of video editing work is done with digital footage and computers. A video editor will usually sit down with the director, and sometimes the producer, and watch hours and hours of raw footage. Together, they will then decide which scenes should be kept and which ones should be deleted. Some shots are deleted for obvious reasons, but others may be deleted, simply because the director didn't like the camera angle. Once all of the final footage has been chosen and melded together, a video editor will then often work with a sound effect editor. Together, they will digitally insert sounds into a movie at just the right moments. The timing has to be perfect during this part of post production, however, since if a sound is just a second or two late, it can ruin the entire effect.

Education Requirements

A minimum of a bachelor's degree in film studies or production is usually necessary in order to start a successful video editing career. While earning these degrees, many students also opt to participate in internships, which allow them to work alongside experienced video editors . Bachelor's degrees will usually be good enough to secure an entry level position as a video editor's assistant. Many aspiring video editors, however, will often

go on to earn master's degrees in video or film editing . Traditional universities will sometimes offer these types of degree programs, but aspiring video editors may want to look into art schools or film schools instead. These types of schools will often be able to offer more specialized training.
SUBJECTS

CAREERS

ACTING

FILM EDITING

SET DESIGN

CASTING DIRECTOR

# 9. Foreign language

Career Options in Foreign Languages
There are plenty of good reasons why to learn a foreign Languages in India. Of all the people I've surveyed, met, taught and listened to over thirteen years, Scope, Job Opportunities & Career Options in Foreign Languages are the single most influential factor in studying a new language.

Introduction
Languages are the central theme of communication in every aspect of human endeavor-be it in the social, economic and political sphere. With modern day Indian emerging as a global player in the socio-economic scheme of things, it has become needful for every individual to be

well equipped with the ability to maintain parity with the rest of the world's multinational and international players. And this can only be achieved through the rudiments of communication which lies in the invaluable process of using multiple languages.

Gone are the days of relying on one's native language in communicating with people, especially in business dealings. The innovative advent of modern technology has made the world a global village, and now, more than ever, the language barrier has to be broken.

To remain competitive and increase your career opportunity and job prospect, you have to communicate smoothly to pave the way for unfettered business connection flows. And here is where learning foreign languages become the new trend in India and offers a wide array of career options in Foreign languages.

Why Learning Foreign Languages is Important in India

People just don't jump in the bandwagon of learning foreign languages in India for the fun of it. With the increase in business interrelationship accelerating globally at an unprecedented rate, Indian companies, firms, and entrepreneurs operating in the country, like Amazon, Infosys, Samsung, TCS, HCL, LG, L&T, IBM, Genpact, Fujitsu Technology, Accenture, and Geometric Ltd, among others, are now evaluating employees on the basis of their foreign language proficiency.

Some of the important incentives of knowing and understanding additional foreign languages involve on-site options, more job openings across various industries, increase the level of salary in comparison to regular graduates, ease of doing business with counterparts and other stakeholders based outside the shores of the country.

If you are looking to earn extra cash from your peers, learn a foreign language. For instance, there was a recent advertisement published on LinkedIn by IBM which states that: "A core developer is needed, with proficiency in French."

You can imagine that. If a renown tech giant like IBM is placing such emphasis on a foreign language as a prerequisite for such an equally important employment, that speaks volume on the importance of learning foreign languages, and while so many Indians these days are taking foreign languages classes.

Following the exploit of globalization, knowing just the mother tongue is no longer enough. Your engineering degree or MBA may no longer earn as much cash as a foreign language would, especially if it is Mandarin, German, French, Japanese, Spanish or Russian.

The entire business environment is currently being driven by a massive requirement for foreign language

experts, translators, trainers, and software developers. To compete competitively and to stand a better chance of realizing your career dream, you have to see the importance of learning a foreign language.
a
Also Read — French DELF Exam in India and TEF, TCF French Exam

The Career Mindset
Of all the people we have surveyed and listened to for the past few years, Career scope and job opportunity in India and abroad is among the most inspiring reason why so many students are learning a foreign language.

We came to discover that there are two main primary categories of people learning foreign languages. These are;

1. People who are learning a foreign language because it offers them a better career opportunity to gain employment.

2. People who start learning a foreign language because of some personal reasons such as migrating to other countries, hobby or interest, travelling, peer group influence, or want to access music, movie, literature in different languages, and then at some point decided it's a good idea to use what they have learned to start a career or to further the objectives of an existing career.

These two classes of reasons can be referred to as "extrinsic and intrinsic" inspiration for foreign language learning.

In India alone, there are about 200 Chinese firms doing business here, and about 5,000 Japanese firms operate here. Currently, more than 2,00,000 people with proficiency in a varied range of language are required for employment opportunities in India. Furthermore, the demand for people with bilingual credibility is on the increase, ranging more than 20% each year.

Also Read — Why Learn Spanish in India? and Why Learn French in India?

Career Options in Foreign Languages
There are many foreign languages available for you to learn. Obviously there are many factors to consider when choosing the right foreign language to learn.

The five of the most famous foreign language options for studies in India are Mandarin Chinese, French, Spanish, German, and Japanese. These languages are regarded as the most sought-after as far as career and prospect, employment opportunities and immigration are concerned.

However, there are other foreign languages in India which are gaining increasing attention from Indian individuals, both at home and abroad. These are Russian, Korean, Portuguese, Italian, Arabic, and others.

Also Read — Benefits of learning french in India , Benefits of learning Spanish in India , Why Learn Japanese? Scope of Mandarin in India, Career after learning korean language and Career in German Language

Career Benefits and Job Opportunities in Foreign Language in India

Academic qualifications and sound proficiency in foreign languages is the key that opens a wider door for a career in vital sectors like tourism, diplomatic services, embassies, journalism, mass communication and public relations, entertainment, arts, publishing, interpretation and translation, public and international organizations. It also affords the opportunity of working with multinationals corporations (MNCs) and governmental specialized agencies.

India is the third fastest growing economy in the world, and there is great expectation that the country will expand its business and bilateral trade links with many countries in Europe, Africa, Latin America, and Asia in the coming years—a process that is already in full swing.

As the country seeks to diversify from reliance on traditional markets like the USA and the UK in the aftermath of the global economic slowdown, thousands of Indian firms are now becoming more proactive—re-strategizing their business outlook across all sectors.

Majority of the Indian businesses are now seeking new business opportunities in Manufacturing, IT, KPO, BPO, Pharmaceuticals, Hospitality, Healthcare, Education, Media, BFSI, and more. While a number of these new markets can boast of essential consumption patterns, English may not be the central language of transition and conversion in these markets.

Thus, knowing a local language in any of these non-English speaking countries is becoming an indispensable factor for Indian firms seeking to do business abroad. These firms need to improve their business, and the only way is to hire personnel with knowledge of the foreign language where their business interest lies.

That explains the continuous rise in demand for employees with foreign languages credentials by Indian businesses trading overseas and non-Indian businesses operating in the country.

Below are some other benefits of learning foreign languages in India.

1. Become a Translator, Interpreter or Teacher
With your knowledge of a foreign language, you can work as a translator or interpreter for a company or as an independent freelancer. There are so many opportunities for translators and

interpreters in India these days, and thanks to the increasing entry of foreign firms and large-scale projects outsourcing to Indian companies by their European and American counterparts.

Acting as an interpreter or a translator can be very lucrative, depending on how experienced you are. You can also work for Media houses, Tourist centers, sports clubs, or such any international company, and so on. Thanks to a plethora of job opportunities, Translator and Interpreter as a Career Options is quite popular among students pursuing language courses.

There are also a career opportunities for editor, proofreader, content writer, teacher, lecturer, and corporate language trainer. The opportunity is just endless.

2. Work for the Immigration / Custom Services

This is one area in which you can flourish handsomely with your knowledge in a foreign language. Foreign Language Jobs in embassy or Government agencies such as the immigration and custom departments will find your resume attractive due to your skills in a foreign language.

Imagine you have a qualification in the Spanish language and the government is out looking for personnel to fill various positions in the nation's embassies in Spanish speaking territories like Latin America and Spain itself. Your resume will definitely receive priority, among other things, ahead of others who don't have such qualification.

Moreover, if you decide to travel or do business in places like Spain or Latin America, your knowledge of Spanish would open up doors of opportunity for you while enabling you to have an equal playing and negotiation dealing with business partners and prospects.

3. Jobs in MNC, KPO, BPO, and IT
ITES (Information Technology Enabled Service), offshoring industry and Outsourcing have brought a lot of job opportunities paving the way for learning foreign languages in India. Adding it to your CV is a surefire way to get a decent job in BPO, KPO, IT and MNC.

Jobs could involve speaking skills, collection of information, working on documents in the corresponding language, voice-based jobs, training, transaction, data processing and migration processes, quality management, email support services, etc.

Indian companies have great expertise in providing a wide range of BPO services across various industry verticals. Multilingual call centre services are offered to various offshore companies in the financial, telecom, medical, insurance and banking sectors.

Today, there is a great demand for foreign language experts in Delhi, Noida, Gurugram, Mumbai, Pune, Bangalore, Hyderabad, Chennai and other parts of the country. The minimum salary range with 0-2 years of experience or Freshers is between 3.5 to 6 lakhs per annum. Foreign language expert salary is generally 25% to 40% higher over their English speaking counterparts.

4. Hospitality & Tourism
There is never a time when people don't move. There is always an exodus of people from different countries of the world to other countries, especially during the holidays and winter seasons.
Millions of people visit India as tourists from year to year. Majority of these people do not speak English nor understand the Indian local dialect.

Attraction centers, shopping malls, 3, 4, and 5-stars hotels & suites need workers that can communicate fluently with these thousands of visitors that patronize their businesses from time to time. With your knowledge in foreign language, you might just be the customer service staff they need. Your multilingual credentials can get you hired just about anywhere that has to do with clients and customers of foreign origin. There are plenty of career options in Travel and Tourism for language learners.

5. Reap big from the Import / Export Sector

The world has become smaller and smaller due to its digitized global economy. These have opened up large opportunity in businesses involving various forms of importation and exportation. Majority of the larger corporations in India now prefer to hire people who can speak new or more foreign languages other than their own native language.

For example, your knowledge of Chinese/Mandarin will open up a career opportunity for you with a firm or company exporting goods or services from India to China, Hong Kong, Taiwan, Mongolia, Malaysia, Philippines, and Thailand. These are the places where the language is spoken as a first or second language. Employers who engage in the export and import business with these countries will find your expertise in Mandarin a huge plus for their businesses.

On the other hand, you might just decide to go solo by doing business with firms and corporations in the aforementioned places — acting as their rep here in India. It is a win-win situation for you any time, and in any place.


Final Thought
The career scope of foreign languages in India is on the rise, and from every indication, the trend will continue until the "alien take over" is complete (pardon my pun). Now that you have known what career reasons and benefits awaits you out there in the corporate world, why don't you start a class in one of

the languages mentioned in this article?

Don't forget, you can't lose out knowing one or more foreign languages; you will always end up the winner. LanguageNext - Centre of Foreign Languages offer a wide range of French, Spanish and Foreign language courses in Noida centre.

## 10. Medical lab technician in U.S.A

A medical laboratory technologist performs complex tests that help other healthcare professionals such as physicians detect, diagnose, and treat diseases. A lab tech who works in a small laboratory typically performs a variety of tests, but one employed in a larger lab is more likely to specialize.

Specialties include histotechnology, immunology, microbiology, and cytogenetic technology. Medical laboratory technologists are also known as laboratory technologists and medical laboratory scientists.

Quick Facts

Medical laboratory technologists earn a median annual salary of $51,770 (2017).
Almost 171,000 people work in this occupation (2016).
Most have jobs in hospitals, diagnostic laboratories, and physicians' offices.
The job outlook for this occupation is excellent. Employment is expected to grow faster than the average for all occupations from 2016 to 2026.

How to Become a Medical Laboratory Technologist
If you want to work in this career, you will need a bachelor's degree in medical laboratory science (MLS).
You can search for a program that has been accredited by the National Accrediting Agency for Clinical Laboratory Sciences (NAACLS) on that organization's website: NAACLS Accredited and Approved Program Search.

Medical laboratory technologists need a license to practice in some states. The Licensed Occupations Tool from CareerOneStop can help you learn what the requirements are where you plan to work. You can also contact that state's health department or board of professional licensing.

Some states and many employers also require professional certification. Credentialing agencies include the American Society of Clinical Pathology (ASCP) Board of Certification and the American Society for Clinical Laboratory Science (ASCLS).

What Soft Skills Do You Need to Succeed in This Career?
In addition to the technical skills you will learn in school and an aptitude for science, you will need the following soft skills—personal qualities you were born with or acquired through life experience—to succeed in this field:

Active Listening: Excellent listening skills will allow you to communicate with patients and fellow medical personnel.

Problem Solving: You must be able to identify problems and solve them.
Critical Thinking: This skill will allow you to determine your options when making decisions or solving problems, compare them, and then choose the one with the most promising outcome.
Attention to Detail: Precision is of the utmost importance when conducting testing procedures.
Reading Comprehension: You must be able to understand and follow physicians' written instructions.

The Truth About Being a Medical Laboratory Technologist
You will have to wear protective equipment and use procedures that mitigate your risk of coming into contact with infectious materials.
If you work in a hospital or other facility that is open 24/7 your work hours may include evenings, overnights, weekends and holidays.
Plan to spend a large part of your day on your feet.
Differences Between a Laboratory Technologist and a Laboratory Technician

Medical laboratory technologist and laboratory technician are related occupations that people often confuse with one another. They differ considerably regarding educational preparation and, subsequently, job duties. Because technologists must earn a bachelor's degree, they have a much more extensive theoretical knowledge base than technicians, who need only an associate degree.

Technicians collect, process, and analyze specimens. They perform lab procedures and maintain instruments. Medical laboratory technologists conduct the same procedures technicians do but also execute sophisticated analyses. They evaluate and interpret the results, conduct research and develop new methods (What is a Medical Laboratory Science Professional. ASCLS: The American Society for Clinical Laboratory Science).

What Will Employers Expect From You? Here are some requirements from job announcements on Indeed.com:

"Ability to work independently and as part of a team"
"Personal computer skills, including strong typing ability and proficient use of Microsoft Office"
"Must be self-motivated and able to prioritize work"
"Must be able to accommodate scheduling adjustments, off shifts, holiday, on-call, and weekend work assignments"
"Ability to deal with problems involving several variables"
"Strong organizational skills"

Is This Occupation a Good Fit for You?

A suitable career matches your personality, interests, and work-related values. A self assessment will let you find out if you have the traits that make this career a good fit. They are:

Interests (Holland Code): IRC (Investigative, Realistic, Conventional)
Personality Type (MBTI Personality Types): ISTJ

Work-Related Values: Support, Independence, Achievement

Related Occupations

| Title | Description | Median Annual Wage (2017) | Minimum Required Education/Training |
|---|---|---|---|
| Pathologist | Analyzes patient specimens to diagnose the presence of diseases | $208,000+ | Doctorate or post-doctoral study |
| Radiologic Technologist | Performs CT scans, x rays, MRIs, and mammograms to help doctors diagnose illnesses and injuries | $58,440 | Associate degree in radiography |
| Phlebotomist | Draws patients' blood | $33,670 | Certificate or diploma from one-year postsecondary phlebotomy training program |
| Nuclear Medicine Technologist | Uses PET and SPECT scans to help doctors diagnose diseases | $75,660 | Associate or bachelor's degree, or 12-month certificate in nuclear medicine technology |

Sources: Bureau of Labor Statistics, U.S. Department of Labor,

Occupational Outlook Handbook; Employment and Training Administration, U.S. Department of Labor, O*NET Online (visited June 18, 2018).

11. Architect

What Architects Do
Architects plan and design houses, factories, office buildings, and other structures.

Duties of Architects

Architects typically do the following:

- Meet with clients to determine objectives and requirements for structures
- Give preliminary estimates on cost and construction time
- Prepare structure specifications
- Direct workers who prepare drawings and documents
- Prepare scaled drawings, either with computer software or by hand
- Prepare contract documents for building contractors
- Manage construction contracts
- Visit worksites to ensure that construction adheres to architectural plans
- Seek new work by marketing and giving presentations

People need places to live, work, play, learn, shop, and eat. Architects are responsible for designing these places. They work on public or private projects and design both indoor and outdoor spaces. Architects can be commissioned to design anything from

a single room to an entire complex of buildings.
Architects discuss the objectives, requirements, and budget of a project with clients. In some cases, architects provide various predesign services, such as feasibility and environmental impact studies, site selection, cost analyses, and design requirements.
Architects develop final construction plans after discussing and agreeing on the initial proposal with clients. The architects' plans show the building's appearance and details of its construction. These plans include drawings of the structural system; air-conditioning, heating, and ventilating systems; electrical systems; communications systems; and plumbing. Sometimes, landscape plans are included as well. In developing designs, architects must follow state and local building codes, zoning laws, fire regulations, and other ordinances, such as those requiring easy access to buildings for people who are disabled.

Architects use computer-aided design and drafting (CADD) and building information modeling (BIM) for creating designs and construction drawings. However, hand-drawing skills are still required, especially during the conceptual stages of a project and when an architect is at a construction site. As construction continues, architects may visit building sites to ensure that contractors follow the design, adhere to the schedule, use the specified materials, and meet work-quality standards. The job is not complete until all construction is finished, required tests are conducted, and construction costs are paid. Architects may also help clients get construction bids, select contractors, and negotiate construction contracts.

Architects often collaborate with workers in related occupations, such as civil engineers, urban and regional
planners, drafters, interior designers, and landscape architects.

Work Environment for Architects

Architects hold about 128,800 jobs. The largest employers of architects are as follows:
Architectural, engineering, and related services
68%
Self-employed workers
20
Government
3
Construction
2

Architects spend much of their time in offices, where they meet with clients, develop reports and drawings, and work with other architects and engineers. They also visit construction sites to ensure clients' objectives are met and to review the progress of projects. Some architects work from home offices.

Architect Work Schedules

Most architects work full time and many work additional hours, especially when facing deadlines. Self-employed architects may have more flexible work schedules.

How to Become an Architect

Get the education you need: Find schools for Architects near you! There are typically three main steps to becoming a licensed architect: completing a bachelor's degree in architecture, gaining relevant experience through a paid internship, and passing the Architect Registration Examination.

Education for Architects

In all states, earning a bachelor's degree in architecture is typically the first step to becoming an architect. Most architects earn their degree through a 5-year Bachelor of Architecture degree program. Many earn a master's degree in architecture, which can take 1 to 5 additional years. The time required depends on the extent of the student's previous education and training in architecture.

A typical bachelor's degree program includes courses in architectural history and theory, building design with an emphasis on computer-aided design and drafting (CADD), structures, construction methods, professional practices, math, physical sciences, and liberal arts.

Currently, 35 states require that architects hold a degree in architecture from one of the 122 schools of architecture accredited by the National Architectural Accrediting Board (NAAB). State licensing requirements can be found at the National Council of Architectural Registration Boards (NCARB).

Training for Architects

All state architectural registration boards require architecture graduates to complete a lengthy paid internship—generally lasting 3 years—before they may sit for the Architect Registration Examination. Most new graduates complete their training period by working at architectural firms through the Architectural Experience Program (AXP), a program run by NCARB that guides students through the internship process. Some states allow a portion of the training to occur in the offices of employers in related careers, such as engineers and general contractors.

Architecture students who complete internships while still in school can count some of that time toward the 3-year training period.

Interns in architectural firms may help design part of a project. They may help prepare architectural documents and drawings, build models, and prepare construction drawings on CADD. Interns may also research building codes and write specifications for building materials, installation criteria, the quality of finishes, and other related details. Licensed architects take the documents that interns produce, make edits to them, finalize plans, and then sign and seal the documents.

Licenses, Certifications, and Registrations for Architects

All states and the District of Columbia require architects to be licensed. Licensing requirements typically include completing a degree program in architecture, gaining relevant experience through a paid internship, and passing the Architect Registration Examination. Most states also require some form of continuing education to keep a license. Continuing education

requirements vary by state but
usually involve additional education
through workshops, university
classes, conferences, self-study
courses, or other sources.
Advancement for Architects
After many years of work experience,
some architects advance to
become architectural and engineering
managers. These managers typically
coordinate the activities of
employees and may work on larger
construction projects.
Important Qualities for Architects
Analytical skills. Architects must
understand the content of designs
and the context in which they were
created. For example, architects
must understand the locations of
mechanical systems and how those
systems affect building operations.
Communication skills. Architects
share their ideas, both in oral
presentations and in writing, with
clients, other architects, and
workers who help prepare drawings.
Many also give presentations to
explain their ideas and designs.
Creativity. Architects design the
overall look of houses, buildings,

and other structures. Therefore, the final product should be attractive and functional.
Organizational skills. Architects often manage contracts. Therefore, they must keep records related to the details of a project, including total cost, materials used, and progress.
Technical skills. Architects need to use CADD technology to create plans as part of building information modeling (BIM).
Visualization skills. Architects must be able to envision how the parts of a structure relate to each other. They also must be able to visualize how the overall building will look once completed.
Architect salary
The median annual wage for architects is $76,930. The median wage is the wage at which half the workers in an occupation earned more than that amount and half earned less. The lowest 10 percent earned less than $46,600, and the highest 10 percent earned more than $129,810.

The median annual wages for architects in the top industries in which they work are as follows:
Government
$88,190
Construction
78,230
Architectural, engineering, and related services
75,910
Most architects work full time and many work additional hours, especially when facing deadlines. Self-employed architects may have more flexible work hours.
Job Outlook for Architect
Employment of architects is projected to grow 4 percent over the next ten years, slower than the average for all occupations. Architects are expected to be needed to make plans and designs for the construction and renovation of homes, offices, retail stores, and other structures. Many school districts and universities are expected to build new facilities or renovate existing ones. In addition, demand is expected for more healthcare facilities as the baby-

boomer population ages and as more people use healthcare services. Demand for architects with a knowledge of "green design," also called sustainable design, is expected to continue. Architects should be needed to design buildings and structures that efficiently use resources, such as energy and water conservation; reduce waste and pollution; and apply environmentally friendly design, specifications, and materials.

Job Prospects for Architects
With a high number of students graduating with degrees in architecture, strong competition for internships and jobs is expected. Employment of architects is strongly tied to the activity of the construction industry. Therefore, these workers may experience periods of unemployment when there is a slowdown in requests for new projects or when the overall level of construction falls.
Employment projections data for Architects, 2016-26
Occupational Title
Employment, 2016

Projected Employment, 2026
Change, 2016-26



Percent
Numeric
Architects, except landscape and naval
128,800
133,900
4
5,100
Careers Related to Architects
Architectural and Engineering Managers
Architectural and engineering managers plan, direct, and coordinate activities in architectural and engineering companies.
Civil Engineers
Civil engineers conceive, design, build, supervise, operate, construct, and maintain infrastructure projects and systems in the public and private sector, including roads, buildings, airports, tunnels, dams, bridges,

and systems for water supply and sewage treatment.

Construction and Building Inspectors
Construction and building inspectors ensure that construction meets local and national building codes and ordinances, zoning regulations, and contract specifications.

Construction Managers
Construction managers plan, coordinate, budget, and supervise construction projects from start to finish.

Drafters
Drafters use software to convert the designs of engineers and architects into technical drawings. Most workers specialize in architectural, civil, electrical, or mechanical drafting and use technical drawings to help design everything from microchips to skyscrapers.

Industrial Designers
Industrial designers develop the concepts for manufactured products, such as cars, home appliances, and toys. They combine art, business, and engineering to make products that people use every day. Industrial designers consider the

function, aesthetics, production costs, and usability of products when developing new product concepts.

Interior Designers

Interior designers make interior spaces functional, safe, and beautiful by determining space requirements and selecting decorative items, such as colors, lighting, and materials. They read blueprints and must be aware of building codes and inspection regulations, as well as universal accessibility standards.

Landscape Architects

Landscape architects design parks and the outdoor spaces of campuses, recreational facilities, businesses, private homes, and other open areas.

Surveying and Mapping Technicians

Surveying and mapping technicians collect data and make maps of the Earth's surface. Surveying technicians visit sites to take measurements of the land. Mapping technicians use geographic data to create maps. They both assist surveyors and cartographers and photogrammetrists.

Surveyors
Surveyors make precise measurements to determine property boundaries. They provide data relevant to the shape and contour of the Earth's surface for engineering, mapmaking, and construction projects.

Urban and Regional Planners
Urban and regional planners develop land use plans and programs that help create communities, accommodate population growth, and revitalize physical facilities in towns, cities, counties, and metropolitan areas.

12. International Business

Read an International Business Job Description: What You'll Do
Airline travel may not be as glamorous today as it was in the 1960s, but a career in international

business will still give motivated globetrotters much to be excited about. Because of the vast and dynamic growth and profit in technology and communication, many corporations are establishing offices overseas.

As a representative for your company in the global arena, you'll enjoy all the responsibilities of businessperson in your field and more. Whether you score an entry level position that incorporates travel or move up to executive or manager status, in international business, you're going places.

Here's an international business job description to help you learn what you can do within this exciting career field.

What education or certification will I need to work in international business?

An associate's degree in international business will get you started on your way, but a bachelor in international business will give you an additional edge.

Many people choose to continue their business education by earning a

Master in Business Administration (MBA), a highly respected advanced degree that indicates a commitment to leading in the field. Your master's will usually take one to two years to obtain. This degree will give you skills that are transferable to other areas of business.

Other advanced degree options are the Master in International Management (MIM) and the Master's in International Business (MIB), which focus almost exclusively on issues related to international business and global management.

Learn more about international business curriculum in What You'll Study.

What does an international businessperson do?

An international business job description definitely includes workers who represent the public face of their companies. They act with knowledge, elegance and cultural sensitivity to facilitate deals and transactions that benefit both parties. All the key elements of success in business at home apply to business abroad: strong leadership skills, implementation of ethical behavior, expertise in your industry and adaptability to evolving technologies.

Common job titles in international business include:
- Import/Export agent
- Translator
- Foreign currency investment advisor
- Foreign sales representative
- International management consultant

Typical employers include banks, import/export corporations, multinational manufacturers, consulting firms, international nongovernmental organizations (NGOs), electronics and technology companies, and transportation industries like shipping and airlines.

What career paths can I take in international business?

With an associate's degree in international business, you'll be ready to work in entry level positions as an international human resources manager, international training manager, international operations manager, accountant, and in taxation and hospitality.

A bachelor's degree is your entrée to the all of those fields plus opportunities in recruitment, sales, brokering customs and executive assisting. Your management opportunities increase exponentially with an MBA, the most popular degree awarded in business. With an MBA and the Master of International Business, you'll be prepared for roles including:

- International marketing director
- Financial controller
- Multinational manager
- Business development director
- International trade and customs manager
- International foreign policy advisor

Learning a new language and keeping up to date on technology will give you a competitive edge.

Those who wish to apply their business knowledge in an academic setting can go on to earn a PhD in international business, which will

open up research, teaching and publishing opportunities.
The U.S. Bureau of Labor Statistics' current Occupational Outlook Handbook places employment growth for interpreters and translators at 29 percent over the next decade, which is much faster than average for all occupations. Job growth for international management analysts should be 14 percent in the same time frame, which is also faster than average. National long-term projections of employment growth may not reflect local and/or short-term economic or job conditions, and do not guarantee actual job growth.

## 13. Dietitian And Nutrionnist

What Dietitians and Nutritionists Do
Dietitians and nutritionists are experts in the use of food and nutrition to promote health and manage disease. They advise people on what to eat in order to lead a healthy lifestyle or achieve a specific health-related goal.
Duties of Dietitians and Nutritionists
Dietitians and nutritionists typically do the following:
- Assess patients' and clients' nutritional and health needs
- Counsel patients on nutrition issues and healthy eating habits
- Develop meal and nutrition plans, taking both clients' preferences and budgets into account
- Evaluate the effects of meal plans and change the plans as needed
- Promote better health by speaking to groups about diet, nutrition, and the relationship between good eating habits and preventing or managing specific diseases

- Create educational materials about healthy food choices
- Keep up with or contribute to the latest food and nutritional science research
- Document patients' progress

Dietitians and nutritionists evaluate the health of their clients. Based on their findings, dietitians and nutritionists advise clients on which foods to eat—and which to avoid—to improve their health.

Many dietitians and nutritionists provide customized information for specific individuals. For example, a dietitian or nutritionist might teach a client with diabetes how to plan meals to balance the client's blood sugar. Others work with groups of people who have similar needs. For example, a dietitian or nutritionist might plan a diet with healthy fat and limited sugar to help clients who are at risk for heart disease. They may work with other healthcare professionals to coordinate patient care.

Dietitians and nutritionists who are self-employed may meet with patients, or they may work as consultants for a variety of organizations. They may need to spend time on marketing and other business-related tasks, such as scheduling appointments, keeping records, and preparing educational programs or informational materials for clients.

Although many dietitians and nutritionists do similar tasks, there are several specialties within the occupations. The following are examples of types of dietitians and nutritionists:

Clinical dietitians and clinical nutritionists provide medical nutrition therapy. They work in hospitals, long-term care facilities, clinics, private practice, and other institutions. They create customized nutritional programs based on the health needs of patients or residents and counsel patients on how to improve their health through nutrition. Clinical dietitians and clinical nutritionists may further specialize, such as by working only with patients with specific conditions such as kidney disease, diabetes, or digestive disorders. Community dietitians and community nutritionists develop programs and counsel the public on topics related to food, health, and nutrition. They often work with specific groups of people, such as adolescents or the elderly. They work in public health clinics, government and nonprofit agencies, health maintenance organizations (HMOs), and other settings.

Management dietitians plan food programs. They work in food service settings such as cafeterias, hospitals, prisons, and schools. They may be responsible for buying food and for carrying out other business-related tasks, such as budgeting. Management dietitians may oversee kitchen staff or other dietitians.

Work Environment for Dietitians and Nutritionists

Dietitians and nutritionists hold about 68,000. The largest employers of dietitians and nutritionists are as follows:

Hospitals; state, local, and private
30%
Government
14
Outpatient care centers
10
Nursing and residential care facilities
9
Self-employed workers
6

Dietitian and Nutritionist Work Schedules

Many dietitians and nutritionists work full time, although about 1 out of 4 work part time. They may work evenings and weekends to meet with clients who are unavailable at other times.

How to Become a Dietitian or Nutritionist

Get the education you need Dietitians and nutritionists typically need a bachelor's degree, along with supervised training through an internship. Many states require dietitians and nutritionists to be licensed.

Education for Dietitians and Nutritionists

Dietitians and nutritionists typically need a bachelor's degree in dietetics, foods and nutrition, clinical nutrition, public health nutrition, or a related area. Dietitians also may study food service systems management. Programs include courses in nutrition, psychology, chemistry, and biology. Many dietitians and nutritionists have advanced degrees.

Dietitian and Nutritionist Training

Dietitians and nutritionists typically receive several hundred hours of supervised training, usually in the form of an internship following graduation from college. Some schools offer coordinated programs in dietetics that allow students to complete supervised training as part of their undergraduate or graduate-level coursework.

Licenses, Certifications, and Registrations for Dietitians and Nutritionists

Many states require dietitians and nutritionists to be licensed in order to practice. Other states require only state registration or

certification to use certain titles, and a few states have no regulations for this occupation.
The requirements for state licensure and state certification vary by state, but most include having a bachelor's degree in food and nutrition or a related area, completing supervised practice, and passing an exam.
Many dietitians choose to earn the Registered Dietitian Nutritionist (RDN) credential. Although the RDN is not always required, the qualifications are often the same as those necessary for becoming a licensed dietitian in states that require a license. Many employers prefer or require the RDN, which is administered by the Commission on Dietetic Registration, the credentialing agency for the Academy of Nutrition and Dietetics.
The RDN requires dietitian nutritionists to complete a minimum of a bachelor's degree and a Dietetic Internship (DI), which consists of at least 1,200 hours of supervised experience. Students may complete both criteria at once

through a coordinated program, or they may finish their required coursework and degree before applying for an internship. These programs are accredited by the Accreditation Council for Education in Nutrition and Dietetics (ACEND), part of the Academy of Nutrition and Dietetics. In order to maintain the RDN credential, dietitians and nutritionists who have earned it must complete 75 continuing professional education credits every 5 years.

Nutritionists may earn the Certified Nutrition Specialist (CNS) credential to show an advanced level of knowledge. The CNS credential or exam is accepted in several states for licensure purposes. To qualify for the credential, applicants must have a master's or doctoral degree, complete 1,000 hours of supervised experience, and pass an exam. The credential is administered by the Board for Certification of Nutrition Specialists. To maintain the CNS credential, nutritionists must complete 75 continuing education credits every 5 years.

Dietitians and nutritionists may seek additional certifications in an area of specialty. The Commission on Dietetic Registration offers several specialty certifications in topics such as oncology nutrition, pediatric nutrition, renal nutrition, and sports dietetics, among others.

Important Qualities for Dietitians and Nutritionists

Analytical skills. Dietitians and nutritionists must keep up to date with the latest food and nutrition research. They should interpret scientific studies and translate nutrition science into practical eating advice.

Compassion. Dietitians and nutritionists must be caring and empathetic when helping clients address health and dietary issues and any related emotions.

Listening skills. Dietitians and nutritionists must listen carefully to understand clients' goals and concerns. They may work with other healthcare workers as part of a team to improve the health of a patient, and they need to listen to team members when constructing eating plans.

Organizational skills. Because there are many aspects to the work of dietitians and nutritionists, they should stay organized. Management dietitians, for example, must consider the nutritional needs of their clients, the costs of meals, and access to food. Self-employed dietitians and nutritionists may need to schedule appointments, manage employees, bill insurance companies, and maintain patient files.

Problem-solving skills. Dietitians and nutritionists must evaluate the health status of patients and determine the most appropriate food choices for a client to improve his or her overall health or manage a disease.

Speaking skills. Dietitians and nutritionists must explain complicated topics in a way that people with less technical knowledge can understand. They must clearly explain eating plans to clients and to other healthcare professionals involved in a patient's care.

Dietitian and Nutritionist Salaries
The median annual wage for dietitians and nutritionists is $58,920. The median wage is the wage at which half the workers in an occupation earned more than that amount and half earned less. The lowest 10 percent earned less than $36,470, and the highest 10 percent earned more than $82,410.

The median annual wages for dietitians and nutritionists in the top industries in which they work are as follows:

Outpatient care centers
$64,880

Hospitals; state, local, and private
59,350

Nursing and residential care facilities
57,330

Government
56,230

Many dietitians and nutritionists work full time, although about 1 out of 4 work part time. They may work evenings and weekends to meet with clients who are unavailable at other times.

Job Outlook for Dietitians and Nutritionists[About this section] [To Top]
Employment of dietitians and nutritionists is projected to grow 14 percent over the next ten years, faster than the average for all occupations. In recent years, interest in the role of food and nutrition in promoting health and wellness has increased, particularly as a part of preventative healthcare in medical settings.

According to the Centers for Disease Control, more than one-third of U.S. adults are obese. Many diseases, such as diabetes and heart disease, are associated with obesity. The importance of diet in preventing and treating illnesses is now well known. More dietitians and nutritionists will be needed to provide care for people with these conditions.

Moreover, as the baby-boom generation grows older and looks for ways to stay healthy, there will be more demand for dietetic and nutrition services. In addition, there will be demand for dietitians

and nutritionists in grocery stores to help consumers make healthy food choices.
Job Prospects for Dietitians and Nutritionists
Dietitians and nutritionists who have earned advanced degrees or certification in a specialty area may enjoy better job prospects.
Employment projections data for Dietitians and Nutritionists, 2016-26
Occupational Title
Employment, 2016
Projected Employment, 2026
Change, 2016-26

Percent
Numeric
Dietitians and nutritionists
68,000
77,600
14
9,600
Careers Related to Dietitians and Nutritionists
Health Educators and Community Health Workers

Health educators teach people about behaviors that promote wellness. They develop and implement strategies to improve the health of individuals and communities. Community health workers collect data and discuss health concerns with members of specific populations or communities.

Registered Nurses

Registered nurses (RNs) provide and coordinate patient care, educate patients and the public about various health conditions, and provide advice and emotional support to patients and their family members.

Rehabilitation Counselors

Rehabilitation counselors help people with physical, mental, developmental, or emotional disabilities live independently. They work with clients to overcome or manage the personal, social, or psychological effects of disabilities on employment or independent living.

14.stenographer

A stenographer, or court reporter, works in the courtroom and transcribes spoken words by typing them into a steno machine, a kind of shorthand typewriter. Fast and accurate typing skills are vital for a stenographer job. Stenographers have to be licensed and certified in addition to passing a special exam.

Essential Information

Stenographers, sometimes called court reporters, are responsible for court and medical transcription and live broadcast captioning for the deaf and elderly. They use shorthand and a steno machine to transcribe information and commit it to the public record. They train through certificate or associate's degree programs and must be fast and accurate typists. Individuals who work in the court system must be licensed and professionally certified in many states.

The U.S. Bureau of Labor Statistics (BLS) predicts that job growth in this field will be slower than average for all occupations through 2024, with the best opportunities for stenographers trained in Communication Access Real-Time Translation (CART) or those who can go with clients to medical appointments or public meetings to provide transcription services.

Required Education
Certificate or associate's degree in court reporting

Other Requirements
Many states require licensure and professional certification

Projected Job Growth (2014-2024)*
2% for all court reporters

Median Salary (2015)*
$49,500 for all court reporters

Sources: *U.S. Bureau of Labor Statistics (BLS).

Stenographer Career Info

Stenographers are responsible for transcribing exact legal or medical proceedings for the record. Stenographers are employed primarily by courts and those in the legal profession, because lawyers and court officials need an exact transcript to use during trials. There is no room for error in the stenography profession, and most in the occupation learn to type at 225 words per minute in order to capture entire conversations quickly and accurately.

Each state has different requirements for stenographers, but all states require stenographers to pass examinations to gain their credentials before they are employed in courts. In most cases, individuals must pass a voice writer test with a written portion covering grammar, spelling and punctuation.

Job Duties

Stenographers must learn a type of shorthand, an abbreviated language form that is designed for rapid transcription, to take notes on a steno machine in order to catch each word that is spoken. Once the notes are entered into the machine by the stenographer, they are translated by computer software into English. The stenographer responsible for recording the proceedings takes the rough transcript and proofreads it before creating a final transcript and committing it to official record. Stenographers must have a good grasp of legal and, for some jobs, medical terminology as well as complete proficiency in the English language to do their jobs to employer standards.

Career Outlook

According to the BLS, the job outlook for stenographers should be slower than the average for all professions. Court reporting was projected to grow by 2% between years 2014-2024. Court reporters with certification were expected to still be in demand, especially in some federal and state courts. Because of growing costs, courts are at times using digital audio recording to replace stenographers, but other markets, such as live captioning for the deaf and elderly, are growing very quickly.

The more efficiently and accurately a stenographer can type, the higher their chances of finding work. Some schools may even offer associate degree programs for stenographers to increase their skills. The job outlook isn't strong, only progressing at 2%, but may increase more in markets like live captioning.

## 15. Dentist

Dentists diagnose and treat problems with a patient's teeth, gums, and related parts of the mouth. They provide advice and instruction on taking care of teeth and gums and on diet choices that affect oral health.

Duties

Dentists typically do the following:
- Remove decay from teeth and fill cavities
- Repair cracked or fractured teeth and remove teeth
- Straighten teeth to correct bite issues
- Place sealants or whitening agents on teeth
- Administer anesthetics to keep patients from feeling pain during procedures
- Write prescriptions for antibiotics or other medications

- Examine x rays of teeth, gums, the jaw, and nearby areas for problems
- Make models and measurements for dental appliances, such as dentures, to fit patients
- Teach patients about diet, flossing, use of fluoride, and other aspects of dental care

Dentists use a variety of equipment, including x-ray machines, drills, mouth mirrors, probes, forceps, brushes, and scalpels. They also use lasers, digital scanners, and other computer technologies.

Dentists in private practice also oversee a variety of administrative tasks, including bookkeeping and buying equipment and supplies. They employ and supervise dental hygienists, dental assistants, dental laboratory technicians, and receptionists.

Most dentists are general practitioners and handle a variety of dental needs. Other dentists practice in one of nine specialty areas:

Dental public health specialists promote good dental

health and the prevention of dental diseases in specific communities.
Endodontists perform root-canal therapy, by which they remove the nerves and blood supply from injured or infected teeth.
Oral and maxillofacial radiologists diagnose diseases in the head and neck through the use of imaging technologies.
Oral and maxillofacial surgeons operate on the mouth, jaws, teeth, gums, neck, and head, including procedures such as surgically repairing a cleft lip and palate or removing impacted teeth.
Oral pathologists diagnose conditions in the mouth, such as bumps or ulcers, and oral diseases, such as cancer.
Orthodontists straighten teeth by applying pressure to the teeth with braces or other appliances.
Pediatric dentists focus on dentistry for children and special-needs patients.
Periodontists treat the gums and bone supporting the teeth.
Prosthodontists replace missing teeth with permanent fixtures, such

as crowns and bridges, or with removable fixtures such as dentures.

Work Environment

Dentists held about 146,800 jobs in 2012. Some dentists own their own businesses and work alone or with a small staff. Other dentists have partners in their practice, and some work for more established dentists as associate dentists.

Dentists usually work in offices. They wear masks, gloves, and safety glasses to protect themselves and their patients from infectious diseases.

Work Schedules

Most dentists work full time. Some work evenings and weekends to meet their patients' needs. The number of hours worked varies greatly among dentists. It is common for dentists to continue in part-time practice well beyond the usual retirement age.

Education and Training

Dentists must be licensed in all states; requirements vary by state. To qualify for a license in most states, applicants must graduate from an accredited dental school and pass written and practical exams.

Education

Most dental students need at least a bachelor's degree before entering dental school; requirements vary by school. All dental schools require applicants to have completed certain required science courses, such as biology and chemistry. Majoring in a science, such as biology, might increase the chances of being accepted, but no specific major is required to enter most dental programs.

College undergraduates who plan on applying to dental school must usually take the Dental Acceptance Test (DAT) during their junior year. Admission to dental school can be competitive. Dental schools use these tests along with other factors, such as grade point average and recommendations, to admit students into their programs.

Dental schools require students to take classes in subjects such as local anesthesia, anatomy, periodontology (the study of oral disease and health), and radiology.

All dental schools include practice where students work with patients in a clinical setting under the supervision of a licensed dentist. High school students who want to become dentists should take courses in chemistry, physics, biology, anatomy, and mathematics.

Training

All nine dental specialties require dentists to complete additional training before practicing that specialty. They must usually complete a 1- or 2-year residency in a program related to their specialty. General dentists do not require any additional training after dental school.

Dentists who want to teach or do research full time usually spend an additional 2 to 5 years in advanced dental training. Many practicing dentists also teach part time, including supervising students in dental school clinics.

Licenses, Certifications, and Registrations

All states require dentists to be licensed; requirements vary by state. Most states require a dentist to have a degree from an accredited dental school and to pass a written and practical exam.

In addition, a dentist who wants to practice in one of the nine specialties must have a license in that specialty. This usually requires 2 to 4 years of additional education after dental school and, in some cases, the completion of a special state exam. A postgraduate residency term also may be required, usually lasting up to 2 years.

Personality and Interests

Dentists typically have an interest in
the Building, Thinking and Helping interest areas, according to
the Holland Codeframework. The Building interest area indicates a focus on working with tools and machines, and making or fixing practical things. The Thinking interest area indicates a focus on researching, investigating, and increasing the understanding of natural laws. The Helping interest area indicates a focus on assisting, serving, counseling, or teaching other people.

If you are not sure whether you have a Building or Thinking or Helping interest which might fit with a career as a dentist, you can take a career test to measure your interests.

Dentists should also possess the following specific qualities:

Communication skills. Dentists must have excellent communication skills. They must be able to communicate effectively with patients, dental hygienists, dental assistants, and receptionists.

Detail oriented. Dentists must be detail oriented so patients receive appropriate treatments and medications. They must also pay attention to space, shape, and color of teeth. For example, they may need to closely match a false tooth with a patient's other teeth.

Dexterity. Dentists must be good at working with their hands. They work with tools in a limited area.

Leadership skills. Most dentists work in their own practice. This requires them to manage and lead a staff.

Organizational skills. Strong organizational skills, including keeping accurate records of patient care, are critical in both medical and business settings.

Patience. Dentists may work for long periods of time with patients who need special attention. Children and patients with a fear of dental work may require a lot of patience.

Physical stamina. Dentists should be comfortable performing physical tasks, such as bending over patients for long periods.

Problem-solving skills. Dentists need strong problem-solving skills. They must evaluate patients' symptoms and choose the appropriate treatments.

Pay

The median annual wage for dentists was $149,310 in May 2012. The median wage is the wage at which half the workers in an occupation earned more than that amount and half earned less. The lowest 10 percent earned less than $73,840, and the top 10 percent earned $187,200 or more. Earnings vary according to the number of years in practice, location, hours worked, and specialty.

The median annual wages for dentists in May 2012 were as follows:
- Equal to or greater than $187,200 for oral and maxillofacial surgeons
- Equal to or greater than $187,200 for orthodontists
- $169,130 for prosthodontists
- $154,990 for dentists, all other specialists
- $145,240 for general dentists

Most dentists work full time. Some work evenings and weekends to meet their patients' needs.

Job Outlook

Employment of dentists is projected to grow 16 percent from 2012 to 2022, faster than the average for all occupations.

Many members of the baby-boom generation will need complicated dental work. In addition, because each generation is more likely to keep their teeth than past generations, more dental care will be needed in the years to come. Dentists will continue to see an increase in public demand for their

services as studies continue to link oral health to overall health.
Dentists are likely to hire more hygienists and dental assistants to handle routine services.
Productivity increases from new technology should allow dentists to reduce the time needed to see each patient. These factors allow the dentist to see more patients when their practices expand.
Dentists will continue to provide care and instruction aimed at promoting good oral hygiene, rather than just providing treatments such as fillings.
Whether patients seek care is largely dependent on their insurance coverage. The number of individuals who have access to health insurance will increase as federal health insurance reform legislation is enacted. People with new or expanded dental insurance coverage will be more likely to visit a dentist than in the past.

Job Prospects

Employment of dentists is not expected to keep pace with the increased demand for dental

services. There are still areas of the country where patients need dental care, but have little access to it. Cosmetic dental services, such as teeth-whitening treatments, will become increasingly popular. This trend is expected to continue as new technologies allow for less invasive, faster procedures.
In addition, many dentists are expected to retire in the next decade and replacement workers will be needed to fill those position

16. Veterinarians

What is a Veterinarian?

MEDIAN SALARY
$90,420
UNEMPLOYMENT RATE

1.7%
NUMBER OF JOBS
15,000
Veterinarians examine, diagnose and treat animals. They can also perform surgeries, care for wounds, vaccinate against diseases and prescribe medications. In worst-case scenarios, vets are also qualified to euthanize sick or dying animals.

Some of the biggest changes Dr. Lorin D. Warnick, dean of the College of Veterinary Medicine at Cornell University, has seen over the course of his career are people's attitudes toward their pets. "Many more people view animals as family members," he says. And that means their expectation for the quality of care is much higher now as well.

Technology in the field has also evolved, Warnick says. Vets are now using everything from advanced surgical technologies to fight cancer to MRIs to care for animals. Genomics are also being used to test for specific genetic traits. But a veterinarian's work doesn't stop with dogs and cats. Some vets specialize in caring for farm animals, and some even protect the safety of our food supply by inspecting livestock. Others promote public health by fighting animal-borne diseases and help foster healthier relationships between people and their animal companions.

The Bureau of Labor Statistics projects 18.8 percent employment growth for veterinarians between 2016 and 2026. In that period, an estimated 15,000 jobs should open up.

Rankings

Veterinarians rank #23 in Best Health Care Jobs. Jobs are ranked according to their ability to offer an elusive mix of factors.

How Much Does a Veterinarian Make?

Veterinarians made a median salary of $90,420 in 2017. The best-paid 25 percent made $118,600 that year, while the lowest-paid 25 percent made $70,810.

25%$70,810Median$90,42075%$118,600

What Type of Education
Do Veterinarians Need?
Although a bachelor's degree isn't a requirement for getting into a Doctor of Veterinary Medicine (D.V.M.) program, most candidates end up having one. And because veterinary medicine is very competitive, it's important to get a solid science background, excellent grades and develop good study habits as an undergraduate student. There are just 30 colleges with accredited D.V.M. programs. These degrees usually take about four years to complete, with the last year reserved for clinical rotations. All states and the District of Columbia require that vets be licensed. They can get their license by graduating from an accredited program and passing the North American Veterinary Licensing Examination. States might also require vets to sit for an additional state exam.

"The financial return is relatively low when compared to the time and cost of education," Warnick says. He recommends taking a close look at one's finances and minimizing student debt as much as possible.

Job Satisfaction

Average Americans work well into their 60s, so workers might as well have a job that's enjoyable and a career that's fulfilling. A job with a low stress level, good work-life balance and solid prospects to improve, get promoted and earn a higher salary would make many employees happy. Here's how Veterinarians job satisfaction is rated in terms of upward mobility, stress level and flexibility.

Upward Mobility
Opportunities for advancements and salary
Above Average

Stress Level
Work environment and complexities of the job's responsibilities
Above Average

Flexibility
Alternative working schedule and work life balance
Below Average

## 17. Tourism

Tourism is a diverse industry which offers long-term career opportunities for enthusiastic individuals who want to put their education and skills to work in various environments. People in tourism may work indoors or outdoors, standard hours or on a flexible schedule, seasonal jobs or all-year-round. It's one of the most exciting and diverse career paths out there.

### What Is Tourism?

The tourism industry can be divided into five career areas: accommodation, food and beverage services, recreation and entertainment, transportation and travel services. All of these areas involve providing services to people who visit BC from other parts of the country and the world.

What Kinds of Careers Are Available in the Tourism Industry?

From operational positions to management and executive-level responsibilities, you'll find opportunities for solid training, knowledge and skill development along with unlimited career growth. The tourism industry also offers a unique environment for those who wish to start their own business.

Operational Positions

These usually involve direct contact with tourists and are often the first step in a lifetime career. Sample jobs include:

- Ski Repair Technician
- Bartender
- Concierge
- Adventure Tour Guide
- Cook
- Sales Coordinator

Supervisory Positions

These people hire, manage, motivate and schedule operational positions as well as provide key functional expertise. Sample jobs include:

- Guest Services Supervisor
- Ski Patrol Supervisor
- Event Planner

- Restaurant Shift Supervisor
- Team Leader Accounting
- Maintenance Supervisor

Management Positions

These positions involve budgeting, analysis, planning and change management in order to help employees and the organization to grow and prosper. There may also be interaction with other tourism sectors and community involvement. Sample jobs include:

- Director of Sales and Marketing
- Head Chef
- Ski Area Manager
- Rooms Division Manager
- Adventure Company Owner
- Attractions Operations Manager

Executives

Executives are often responsible for several departments or divisions and usually work at a regional, national or international level. They are responsible for strategic planning and have significant budget responsibility. Sample jobs include:

- Hotel General Manager
- Regional Manager of Restaurant Chain
- Vice President of Human Resources

- Tour Company President
- Convention Centre Executive Director
- CEO of Destination Marketing Organization (e.g. Tourism British Columbia)

There are also many opportunities for entrepreneurs in the tourism industry. Whether you're looking to open a resort, an eco-tourism outfit, an adventure operation or a bed and breakfast, the incredible growth of tourism in BC means plenty of business opportunities for the entrepreneurial minded.

How Much Will I Make?

Salary ranges in tourism jobs depend on the type of job you're doing , the amount of education and training required, and your experience level. Keep in mind that many people in tourism careers also make tips on top of their salary. Also, 77% of BC tourism organizations offer extended health care, 74% offer employees life insurance, 73% offer long-term disability and 81% offer dental care.

Here are a few sample average wages for various tourism positions in BC:
Hotel General Manager
$40,000 - $90,000 / yr
Accommodations Service Manager
$36,601 - $59,160 / yr
Executive Chef
$45,000 - $71,386 / yr
Director of Sales and Marketing
$48,580 - $80,000 / yr
Executive Housekeeper
$34,000 - $50,000 / yr
Banquet Server
$9.00 - $13.74 / hr
Concierge
$13.77 - $17.46 / hr
Front Desk Agent
$10.25 - $17.31 / hr
Guest Service Attendant
$10.25 - $13.50 / hr
Housekeeping Room Attendant
$10.25 - $16.75 / hr

## 18. Radiologic and MRI technologist

### What Radiologic and MRI Technologists Do

Radiologic technologists, also known as radiographers, perform diagnostic imaging examinations, such as x rays, on patients. MRI technologists operate magnetic resonance imaging (MRI) scanners to create diagnostic images.

### Duties of Radiologic and MRI Technologists

Radiologic and MRI technologists typically do the following:
- Adjust and maintain imaging equipment
- Precisely follow orders from physicians on what areas of the body to image
- Prepare patients for procedures, including taking a medical history and answering questions about the procedure

- Protect the patient by shielding exposed areas that do not need to be imaged
- Position the patient and the equipment in order to get the correct image
- Operate the computerized equipment to take the images
- Work with physicians to evaluate the images and to determine whether additional images need to be taken
- Keep detailed patient records

Healthcare professionals use many types of equipment to diagnose patients. Radiologic technologists specialize in x-ray and computed tomography (CT) imaging. Some radiologic technologists prepare a mixture for the patient to drink that allows soft tissue to be viewed on the images that the radiologist reviews.

Radiologic technologists might also specialize in
mammography. Mammographers use low-dose x-ray systems to produce images of the breast. Technologists may be certified in multiple specialties. MRI technologists specialize in magnetic resonance imaging scanners.

They inject patients with contrast dyes so that the images will show up on the scanner. The scanners use magnetic fields in combination with the contrast agent to produce images that a physician can use to diagnose medical problems.

Healthcare professionals who specialize in other diagnostic equipment include nuclear medicine technologists and diagnostic medical sonographers, and cardiovascular technologists and technicians, including vascular technologists.

Work Environment for Radiologic and MRI Technologists

Magnetic resonance imaging technologists hold about 36,600 jobs. The largest employers of magnetic resonance imaging technologists are as follows:

Hospitals; state, local, and private 59%

Medical and diagnostic laboratories 20

Offices of physicians 13

Outpatient care centers 4

Radiologic technologists hold about

205,200 jobs. The largest employers of radiologic technologists are as follows:

Hospitals; state, local, and private 59%
Offices of physicians 20
Medical and diagnostic laboratories 8
Outpatient care centers 6
Federal government, excluding postal service 3

Radiologic and MRI technologists are often on their feet for long periods and may need to lift or turn patients who are disabled.

Injuries and Illnesses for Radiologic and MRI Technologists

Like other healthcare workers, radiologic and MRI technologists may be exposed to infectious diseases. In addition, because radiologic technologists work with imaging equipment that uses radiation, they must wear badges that measure radiation levels in the radiation area. Detailed records are kept on their cumulative lifetime dose.

Although radiation hazards exist in this occupation, they are minimized by the use of protective lead aprons, gloves, and other shielding devices, and by badges that monitor exposure to radiation.

Radiologic and MRI Technologist Work Schedules

Most radiologic and MRI technologists work full time. Because imaging is sometimes needed in emergency situations, some technologists work evenings, weekends, or overnight.

How to Become a Radiologic or MRI Technologist

Get the education you need: Find schools for Radiologic and MRI Technologists near you!

Radiologic technologists and MRI technologists typically need an associate's degree. Many MRI technologists start out as radiologic technologists and specialize later in their career. Radiologic technologists must be licensed or certified in most states. Few states license MRI technologists. Employers typically require or prefer prospective technologists to be certified even if the state does not require it.

Education for Radiologic and MRI Technologists

An associate's degree is the most common educational requirement for radiologic and MRI technologists. There also are postsecondary education programs that lead to graduate certificates or bachelor's degrees. Education programs typically include both classroom study and clinical work. Coursework includes anatomy, pathology, patient care, radiation physics and protection, and image evaluation. The Joint Review Committee on Education in Radiologic Technology (JRCERT) accredits programs in radiography and the American Registry of Magnetic Resonance Imaging Technologists (ARMRIT) accredits MRI programs. Completing an accredited program is required for licensure in some states.

High school students who are interested in radiologic or MRI technology should take courses that focus on math and science, such as anatomy, biology, chemistry, physiology, and physics.

Work Experience in a Related Occupation for Radiologic and MRI Technologists

MRI technologists typically have less than 5 years of work experience as radiologic technologists.

Licenses, Certifications, and Registrations for Radiologic and MRI Technologists

Radiologic technologists must be licensed or certified in most states. Few states license MRI technologists. Requirements vary by state.

To become licensed, technologists must usually graduate from an accredited program, and pass a certification exam from the state or obtain a certification from a certifying body. Certifications for radiologic technologists are available from the American Registry of Radiologic Technologists (ARRT). Certifications for MRI technologists are available from the ARRT and from the American Registry of Magnetic Resonance Imaging Technologists (ARMRIT). For specific licensure requirements for radiologic technologists and MRI technologists, contact the state's health board. Employers typically require or prefer prospective technologists to be certified even if the state does not require it.

Important Qualities for Radiologic and MRI Technologists

Detail oriented. Radiologic and MRI technologists must follow exact instructions to get the images needed for diagnoses.

Interpersonal skills. Radiologic and MRI technologists work closely with patients who may be in extreme pain or mentally stressed. They must put the patient at ease to get usable images.

Math skills. Radiologic and MRI technologists may need to calculate and mix the right doses of chemicals used in imaging procedures.

Physical stamina. Radiologic and MRI technologists often work on their feet for long periods during their shift and they must lift and move patients who need assistance.

Technical skills. Radiologic and MRI technologists must understand how to operate complex machinery.

Radiologic and MRI Technologist Salaries

The median annual wage for magnetic resonance imaging technologists is $68,420. The median wage is the wage at which half the workers in an occupation earned more than that amount and half earned less. The lowest 10 percent earned less than $47,960, and the highest 10 percent earned more than $95,890.

The median annual wage for radiologic technologists is $57,450. The lowest 10 percent earned less than $38,660, and the highest 10 percent earned more than $82,590

19. Pilot

How to Become a Pilot?
To have a training for pilot, one should have passed 10+2 or equivalent exam with Physics, chemistry and Mathematics. For admission, there is a written test

that comprises test papers like English, maths, physics, reasoning, general awareness and current affairs. The minimum age to get enroll in a pilot training institute is 17 years. One has to fulfill the medical standard as prescribed by the Directorate General of Civil Aviation (DGCA). The training fee is Rs 25 lakh and involves 200 hours of flying training. The duration of the course is 15-18 months. There are institutes in India, which are offering pilot training in India

- Indira Gandhi Rashtriya Uran Akademi, Rae Bareli (IGRU) (wwww.igrua.gov.in)
- Orient Flight School, Chennai (www.orientflights.com)
- Puducherry Thakur College of Aviation
- Institute of Aviation and Aviation Safety

Pilots Duties and Works

In the cockpit, there are two pilots. The experienced one is the captain and other is the co-pilot. In bigger aircraft, there is a third pilot too who is known as the flight engineer. However, after the

automatic computerized monitoring system, maximum airlines are left with only two pilots. The captain keep surveillance to other crew members while co-pilot monitoring the system and communicate with the air traffic controllers. The different functions of air pilots are:
• Checking the aircraft so to make its smooth functioning
• To know about weather condition of all the destinations en route.
• Keep a hawk eye on speed, altitude and instrument flight rules. Instrument flight rule is used during poor visibility to make coordination with air traffic controllers.
• To take utmost care during takeoff and landing.
• Helicopter pilots should be careful of transmission towers and power lines.
How do Pilots fly Aircraft?
To fly aeroplane, the significance of manual work is minimal. A great part of the work is being executed with the help of powerful automatic-controlled computer whose

works are being monitored by the pilot. The pilot observed the navigational and communication systems, be prepared about weather changes and always keep in touch with air traffic controller. Pilots are generally recruited for commercial airlines, but they are also hired by army and also show their calibre in helicopter flying.

Pilot Aircraft Training

For pilot training, the candidate initially is given Student Pilot License. This training is followed by Private Pilot License where the pilot captained a aircraft without passengers. The advanced form of training is Commercial Pilot License where the pilot fly the aircraft along with passengers. This CPL is provided by Directorate General of Civil Aviation.

To be a successful pilot, one need a certificate of commercial pilot with logging of 250 flight hours. Besides these criteria, to become a versatile pilot, one may initially try for flight instruction, pipeline patrol, flying traffic watch and skydive pilot. These may be fruitful to become a good pilot for airlines. In India, the cost of pilot training is Rs 30 lakh, sometime reached to one crore as per the specialisation while in US, it is about 25 lakh. In US or developed countries, training for CPL is less than India because of high cost fuel and imposed duties as explained by the Indian system. Every time a pilot wants to upgrade for a bigger aircraft, he has to pay additional amount Rs 25 to 30 lakh.

Even after become a pilot, one have to pass medical fitness test after every six months.

Jobs in Airline Sectors

Jobs growth are comparatively better in the airlines sector. Both economic as well as population growth give boost to the airline sector. Since, the regional airlines are growing faster, so have the higher jobs opportunity. From Job points of view, airline sector is hot cake. The soaring salaries and visiting to the different destinations fascinates everyone. Though, the initial fees is quite high, yet with the availability of loans, getting admission into aircraft institute is no more the dream. After the CPL, the candidate gets job in airline as co-pilot. At the major airlines, which offer handsome salary and other benefits, the competition of pilots are fierce. However, best opportunities are available for pilots at low cost airlines. In US, the package for pilots varies from $56, 000 to $106, 000

Airlines Job Opportunities Abroad

To be commercial pilot in India, one should have a flying experience of 250 hours while in case of developed countries, the situation is not so. In countries like Europe, to have a basic licence experience, one have a flying experience of 750 hours. In foreign countries, the package is double to India. Sometimes, the pay is thrice or 4 times than India. On the other hand, these countries also made available lucrative avenues for the pilots. There is a more job certainty and satisfaction in abroad pilot jobs.

Airline Recession

Economy recession has made a greater impact on the recruitment procedures of airlines. About 6, 000 pilots are unemployed in India and after every six months, about 600 pilots re joined them. Since, the candidates joined for pilot just after 12th class, so, alternative career opportunities is limited. After spending Rs 30 lakh for commercial pilot training, and searching jobs for months and years is quite depressing both for the candidates and the parents. All the aspiring candidates are suggested to must have second option so that even in the diminishing phase, the candidates should not be worried more.

20.software developer

What Software Developers Do
Software developers are the creative minds behind computer programs. Some develop the applications that allow people to do specific tasks on a computer or another device. Others develop the underlying systems that run the devices or that control networks.
Duties of Software Developers
Software developers typically do the following:
• Analyze users' needs and then design, test, and develop software to meet those needs
• Recommend software upgrades for customers' existing programs and systems
• Design each piece of an application or system and plan how the pieces will work together

- Create a variety of models and diagrams (such as flowcharts) that show programmers the software code needed for an application
- Ensure that a program continues to function normally through software maintenance and testing
- Document every aspect of an application or system as a reference for future maintenance and upgrades
- Collaborate with other computer specialists to create optimum software

Software developers are in charge of the entire development process for a software program. They may begin by asking how the customer plans to use the software. They must identify the core functionality that users need from software programs. Software developers must also determine user requirements that are unrelated to the functions of the software, such as the level of security and performance needs. They design the program and then give instructions to programmers, who write computer code and test it.

If the program does not work as expected or if testers find it too difficult to use, software developers go back to the design process to fix the problems or improve the program. After the program is released to the customer, a developer may perform upgrades and maintenance.

Developers usually work closely with computer programmers. However, in some companies, developers write code themselves instead of giving instructions to programmers.

Developers who supervise a software project from the planning stages through implementation sometimes are called information technology (IT) project managers. These workers monitor the project's progress to ensure that it meets deadlines, standards, and cost targets. IT project managers who plan and direct an organization's IT department or IT policies are included in the profile on computer and information systems managers.

The following are examples of types of software developers:

Applications software developers design computer applications, such as word

processors and games, for consumers. They may create custom software for a specific customer or commercial software to be sold to the general public. Some applications software developers create complex databases for organizations. They also create programs that people use over the Internet and within a company's intranet.
Systems software developers create the systems that keep computers functioning properly. These could be operating systems for computers that the general public buys or systems built specifically for an organization. Often, systems software developers also build the system's interface, which is what allows users to interact with the computer. Systems software developers create the operating systems that control most of the consumer electronics in use today, including those used by cell phones and cars.
Work Environment for Software Developers
Software developers, applications hold about 831,300 jobs. The largest

employers of software developers, applications are as follows:

Computer systems design and related services
35%

Software publishers
10

Finance and insurance
10

Manufacturing
7

Management of companies and enterprises
5

Software developers, systems software hold about 425,000 jobs. The largest employers of software developers, systems software are as follows:

Computer systems design and related services
31%

Manufacturing
18

Software publishers
6

Finance and insurance
6

Engineering services
4

In general, software development is a collaborative process, and developers work on teams with others who also contribute to designing, developing, and programming successful software. However, some developers work at home.

Software Developer Work Schedules

Most software developers work full time, and additional work hours are common.

How to Become a Software Developer

Education for Software Developers

Software developers usually have a bachelor's degree, typically in computer science, software engineering, or a related field. Computer science degree programs are the most common, because they tend to cover a broad range of topics. Students should focus on classes related to building software to better prepare themselves for work in the occupation. Many students gain experience in software development by completing an internship at a software company while in college. For some positions, employers may prefer that applicants have a master's degree.

Although writing code is not their first priority, developers must have a strong background in computer programming. They usually gain this experience in school. Throughout their career, developers must keep up to date on new tools and computer languages.

Software developers also need skills related to the industry in which they work. Developers working in a bank, for example, should have knowledge of finance so that they can understand a bank's computing needs.

Advancement for Software Developers

Software developers can advance to become information technology (IT) project managers, also called computer and information systems managers, a position in which they oversee the software development process.

Important Qualities for Software Developers

Analytical skills. Developers must analyze users' needs and then design software to meet those needs.

Communication skills. Developers must be able to give clear

instructions to others working on a project. They must also explain to their customers how the software works and answer any questions that arise.
Creativity. Developers are the creative minds behind new computer software.
Detail oriented. Developers often work on many parts of an application or system at the same time and must therefore be able to concentrate and pay attention to detail.
Interpersonal skills. Software developers must be able to work well with others who contribute to designing, developing, and programming successful software.
Problem-solving skills. Because developers are in charge of software from beginning to end, they must be able to solve problems that arise throughout the design process.
The median annual wage for applications software developers is $100,080. The median wage is the wage at which half the workers in an occupation earned more than that amount and half earned less. The lowest 10 percent earned less than

$58,300, and the highest 10 percent earned more than $157,590.
The median annual wage for systems software developers is $106,860. The lowest 10 percent earned less than $64,650, and the highest 10 percent earned more than $163,220.
The median annual wages for applications software developers in the top industries in which they work are as follows:
Software publishers
$111,250
Manufacturing
107,280
Finance and insurance
101,520
Management of companies and enterprises
98,020
Computer systems design and related services
97,720
The median annual wages for systems software developers in the top industries in which they work are as follows:
Manufacturing
$117,360
Engineering services

110,760
Finance and insurance
108,720
Computer systems design and related services
105,250
Software publishers
104,040
Most software developers work full time, and additional work hours are common.
Job Outlook for Software Developers
Employment of software developers is projected to grow 24 percent over the next ten years, much faster than the average for all occupations. Employment of applications developers is projected to grow 30 percent, and employment of systems developers is projected to grow 11 percent. The main reason for the growth in both applications developers and systems developers is a large increase in the demand for computer software.
The need for new applications on smart phones and tablets will help increase the demand for applications software developers.

The health and medical insurance and reinsurance carriers industry will need innovative software to manage new healthcare policy enrollments and administer existing policies digitally. As the number of people who use this digital platform increases over time, demand for software developers will grow. Systems developers are likely to see new opportunities because of an increase in the number of products that use software. For example, more computer systems are being built into consumer electronics and other products, such as cell phones and appliances.

Concerns over threats to computer security could result in more investment in security software to protect computer networks and electronic infrastructure. In addition, an increase in software offered over the Internet should lower costs and allow more customization for businesses, also increasing demand for software developers.

Job Prospects for Software Developers

Job prospects will be best for applicants with knowledge of the most up-to-date programming tools and for those who are proficient in one or more programming languages. Employment projections data for Software Developers, 2016-26

Occupational Title

Employment, 2016

Projected Employment, 2026

Change, 2016-26

Percent

Numeric

Software developers

1,256,200

1,555,700

24

299,500

Software developers, applications

831,300

1,084,600

30

253,400

Software developers, systems software

425,000

471,000

46,100

Careers Related to Software Developers

Computer and Information Research Scientists

Computer and information research scientists invent and design new approaches to computing technology and find innovative uses for existing technology. They study and solve complex problems in computing for business, medicine, science, and other fields.

Computer and Information Systems Managers

Computer and information systems managers, often called information technology (IT) managers or IT project managers, plan, coordinate, and direct computer-related activities in an organization. They help determine the information technology goals of an organization and are responsible for implementing computer systems to meet those goals.

Computer Hardware Engineers

Computer hardware engineers research, design, develop, and test

computer systems and components such as processors, circuit boards, memory devices, networks, and routers.
Computer Network Architects
Computer network architects design and build data communication networks, including local area networks (LANs), wide area networks (WANs), and Intranets. These networks range from small connections between two offices to next-generation networking capabilities such as a cloud infrastructure that serves multiple customers.
Computer Programmers
Computer programmers write and test code that allows computer applications and software programs to function properly. They turn the program designs created by software developers and engineers into instructions that a computer can follow.
Computer Support Specialists
Computer support specialists provide help and advice to computer users and organizations. These specialists either support computer networks or

they provide technical assistance directly to computer users.

## Computer Systems Analysts

Computer systems analysts, sometimes called systems architects, study an organization's current computer systems and procedures, and design solutions to help the organization operate more efficiently and effectively. They bring business and information technology (IT) together by understanding the needs and limitations of both.

## Database Administrators

Database administrators (DBAs) use specialized software to store and organize data, such as financial information and customer shipping records. They make sure that data are available to users and secure from unauthorized access.

## Information Security Analysts

Information security analysts plan and carry out security measures to protect an organization's computer networks and systems. Their responsibilities are continually expanding as the number of cyberattacks increases.

## Mathematicians and Statisticians

Mathematicians and statisticians analyze data and apply mathematical and statistical techniques to help solve real-world problems in business, engineering, healthcare, or other fields.

Postsecondary Teachers

Postsecondary teachers instruct students in a wide variety of academic and technical subjects beyond the high school level. They may also conduct research and publish scholarly papers and books.

Web Developers

Web developers design and create websites. They are responsible for the look of the site. They are also responsible for the site's technical aspects, such as its performance and capacity, which are measures of a website's speed and how much traffic the site can handle. In addition, web developers may create content for the site.

www.ingramcontent.com/pod-product-compliance
Lightning Source LLC
Chambersburg PA
CBHW021824170526
45157CB00007B/2676